WILLOW WEAVING

Truus Stol & Janny Roelofsen

SEARCH PRESS

First published in Great Britain 2004
Search Press Limited
Wellwood
North Farm Road
Tunbridge Wells
Kent TN2 3DR

Originally published in The Netherlands
2002 by Forte Uitgevers, Utrecht
© Forte Uitgevers bv, Boothstraat 1c,
3512 BT Utrecht

English translation by Janet Wilson
English translation copyright © Search
Press Limited 2004

ISBN 1 84448 015 1

Front cover: Studio Herman Bade BV,
Baarn
Photography: Jennie Schotman Fotografie
Illustrations: Irene van den Bos
Editing: Olga Dol
Design: Studio Herman Bade BV, Baarn
Publisher: Koos van Beusekom
Adviser: Gert van Zandbergen
Support: Olga Dol

With thanks to: Kars & Co BV, Ochten
Florabase, Rijnsburg

Contents

Foreword

'Willow withes, also known as rods or osiers, are used for all the projects in this book. They are specially cultivated stems which are cut each year between the months of November and April.

The fifteen projects are inspired by animals and the seasons. The first models we created were lovely round-bodied pigs. Since then our collection of animals has grown considerably. We also love making decorative models and, inspired by the seasons have created many objects, from Spring garlands and baskets to summer boats and festive lamps.

We hope you are as inspired as we are with the beauty of willow, and we wish you many hours of happy and successful weaving.'

Truus Stol and Janny Roelofsen

Storing willow

Rods are flexible and easy to work with when they have just been cut, but if you plan to store them for some time, it is advisable to soak them before use. They are best stored under a lean-to or porch out of the rain, so that the wind blows through them. Rods should only be soaked once, as repeated soakings will remove the bark.

Once the model has been made, protect it from weathering by coating it with garden furniture oil.

BASIC TECHNIQUES

*Master the technique of how to weave rings and
you have the basis for every project.*

Woven ring

All the projects are created from basic woven rings which are then formed
into the shapes shown in the illustrations and photographs. The rod lengths
required for each model are listed in the materials boxes throughout the
book and below is a list of the materials you will need for each project.
Always use the whole length of the rods; do not be tempted to cut them.
You will be given a circumference measurement for each project which is the
outer side of the formed ring.

To make a basic ring, bend the rod round to the desired size and weave
the ends as shown (a). Wrap the second rod around the ring as shown (b),
and then the third, always working in the same direction. The fourth rod is
wound round the circle in the opposite direction.

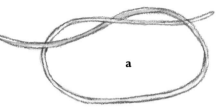

bend the rod round and weave in the ends

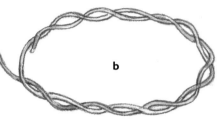

wrap the second rod around the ring
working in the same direction

Making the ring

Several rings can be used to make one model and these are bound
together with garden wire to create the desired shape. Once
the rings are bound, a foundation is made for the weaving
process by pushing the thicker end of a rod through an
opening in one of the rings, from the inside of the circle, outwards (c).
This is repeated until the basic frame for the model is formed.

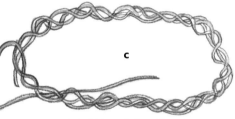

push the thicker end of a rod through an
opening in the ring

Materials

Rods 120cm (47¼in)

Rods 175cm (69in)

Secateurs

Awl

Garden wire

Wire cutter

Glue gun

Tape measure

TABLE BASKET

A basket makes a beautiful garden table decoration. Woven willow leaves are formed into fantasy flowers and filled with soft, green moss and colourful plants.

Materials

Bundle of rods, 120cm (47¼in)

Metal stand

Moss

Wire mesh lining

Garden wire

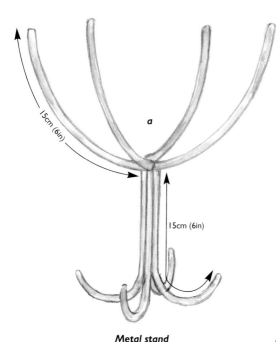

Metal stand

You will need to buy a metal stand for this project. We have used a cup-shaped stand, as shown in diagram (a). Make a 65cm (25½in) ring (see page 5) and bend this into a leaf shape. Weave rods into the leaf frame, as shown in the photograph. Repeat the process and make five leaves. Bind each one to the inside of the stand using garden wire, then join each of them together by weaving rods from the bottom to halfway up the stand, as shown below (b). Lay moss (mossy side out) into this basket and line with wire mesh. Fill the basket with earth and plants.

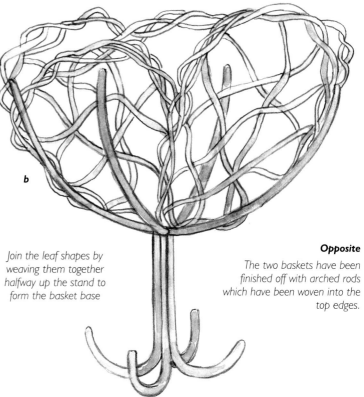

Join the leaf shapes by weaving them together halfway up the stand to form the basket base

Opposite

The two baskets have been finished off with arched rods which have been woven into the top edges.

SPRING BASKET

These beautiful baskets can be filled to the brim with flowers and decorations throughout the year. Plant yellow flowers in the Spring, blue and red flowers in the Summer and make an Autumn arrangement of gourds, dried leaves, seeds and dried flowers as winter approaches.

Materials

¼ bundle of rods, 120cm (47¼in)
Wire mesh for sides, 10 x 100cm
(4 x 39½in)
Wire mesh oval for base, 25 x 35cm
(9¾ x 13¾in)
Garden wire
Moss

Weave two strong rings (see page 5) and bend them into ovals. These will form the top and bottom of the basket.

Bend the wire mesh for the sides round, overlapping the two ends by 10cm (4in). Secure these ends together with garden wire, then bind the wire mesh base into place.

Place one of the woven rings around the wire mesh base and secure it with garden wire. Place the other ring around the top of the basket and secure. Weave a rod over each ring and through the wire. To form a handle, weave a 15cm (6in) loop, leaving a distance of 10cm (4in) between the two ends, and secure with garden wire. Repeat on the opposite side.

Finally, lay the moss inside the basket, against the wire mesh and around the sides. Fill the basket with flowers, pots and willow rods.

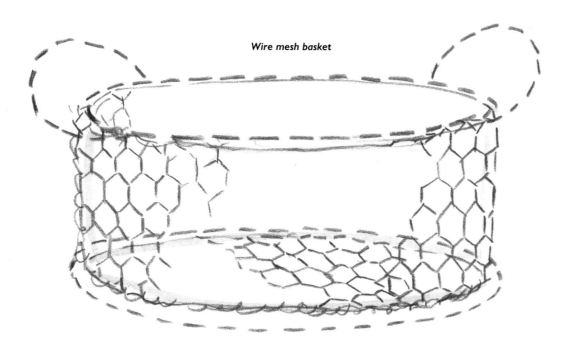

Wire mesh basket

EASTER GARLAND

Everyone loves spring, with fresh green shoots, yellow daffodils and primroses bursting through the earth to herald the warmer weather. This garland, adorned with soft feathers, ribbons and leaves, can be attached to a door to welcome family, friends and visitors, or display it on your garden table as a stunning centrepiece.

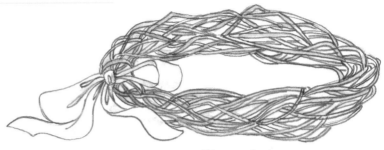

Woven garland

Using the basic woven ring as a base (see page 5), make a circle with a circumference of 90cm (35½in). To create a simple garland, continue weaving the rods until the ring is 25cm (9½in) thick, twisting them in alternate directions, one to the left, the next to the right, to produce a fuller shape.

For the table garland shown here, make a base inside the garland: weave rods from left to right to form the foundation, then weave more in to fill in the gaps. Shape the dried grasses into a nest, then fill it with hay, hand-crafted painted eggs and a few feathers. For the door garland, make a smaller nest and fill it with spring foliage, then tie a yellow ribbon around the top.

Materials

¼ bundle of rods, 120cm (47¼in)
¼ bundle of rods, 175cm (69in)
Dried grasses
Hay
Feathers
Hand crafted painted eggs
Yellow ribbon
Bay sprigs
Garden wire

Bird's body

Middle ring, circumference 23cm (9in)
Oval, circumference 28cm (11in)

Bird's head

Round ring, circumference 8cm (3in)
Round ring, circumference 9cm (3½in)

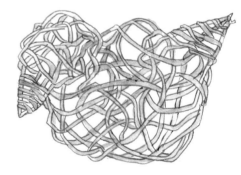

four rings are used as a base for the weaving

Bird

Make the two rings for the body. Shape one into an oval, then place the two together with the ring in the middle and the oval cross-wise to form the body. Bind them with wire. Using one rod, weave one end closed. Using the two smaller rings, form a foundation and then the head. The beak is 1.5cm (½in) long. Position the head, as shown above. To form the body, weave the remaining rods into the oval and ring to form a frame, then weave the body. The tail is 4cm (1½in) long and 2cm (¾in) wide. Make two birds and place them in the nests as shown opposite.

Fantasy Birds

These small, slender birds look wonderful framed against the light on a windowsill. With their inquisitive expressions and playful poses they make delightful, natural ornaments.

Weave four basic rings (see Materials list below) and shape them into ovals. Place the large inner oval crosswise inside the large outer oval and secure with wire. Secure the two smaller inner ovals upright within the shape, as shown below, and secure them to the two outer ovals with wire. Using several rods, make a frame to work on (see page 5) then select more rods and weave them into shape to form the body, working from the bottom up and leaving a 10cm (4in) gap in the centre, beneath the body, for the legs. To make the tail, form a point at the rear.

Keep the weaving as flat as possible.

To form a base for the neck and head, attach the electrical wire to the body, as shown below, and bend it into shape. Weave a rod on to this wire, working from the body, up to the end of the beak and back. Repeat this with a second rod, but this time, when turning back curve it down to the neck to form the head. Keep weaving rods into the head until it is finished. Finally, push the metal legs into the body.

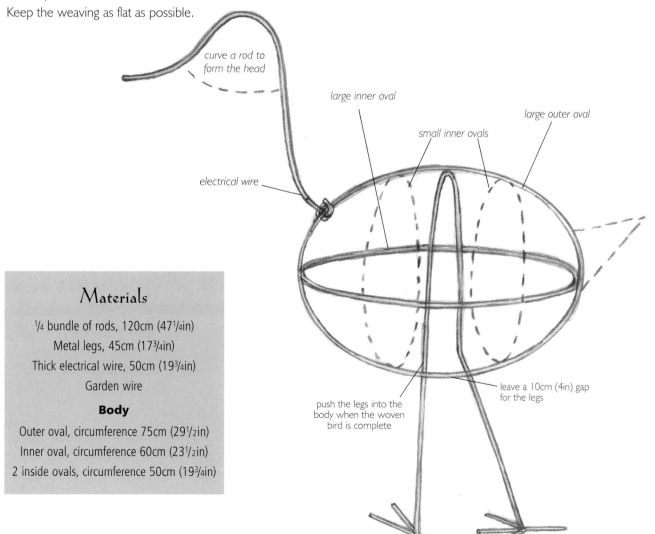

curve a rod to form the head

large inner oval

large outer oval

small inner ovals

electrical wire

leave a 10cm (4in) gap for the legs

push the legs into the body when the woven bird is complete

Materials

¼ bundle of rods, 120cm (47¼in)
Metal legs, 45cm (17¾in)
Thick electrical wire, 50cm (19¾in)
Garden wire

Body

Outer oval, circumference 75cm (29½in)
Inner oval, circumference 60cm (23½in)
2 inside ovals, circumference 50cm (19¾in)

13

BUTTERFLIES

These butterflies appear to be sunbathing as they enjoy the flowers and plants that line the path. They are an attractive feature in this tranquil corner of the garden.

Materials

¼ bundle of rods, 120cm (47¼in)

Garden wire

Wings

2 top rings, circumference
65cm (25½in)

2 bottom rings, circumference
60cm (23½in)

Make four basic woven rings (see page 5) and bind the two larger top rings to the two smaller bottom rings with garden wire. Bend them to resemble wings. Make a rod framework within the four shapes, then weave more rods into the wings as shown in the photograph. To make the body which has a total length of 30cm (11¾in) (see diagram below), bend two rods almost double lengthways. Shape the body with more rods, making the head a little larger, so that its circumference is 25cm (9¾in). Secure the wings to the body with rods, weaving them in and around to create a realistic shape. Finally, push two 8cm (3in) rods into the head for the antennae, and knot a rounded end on each.

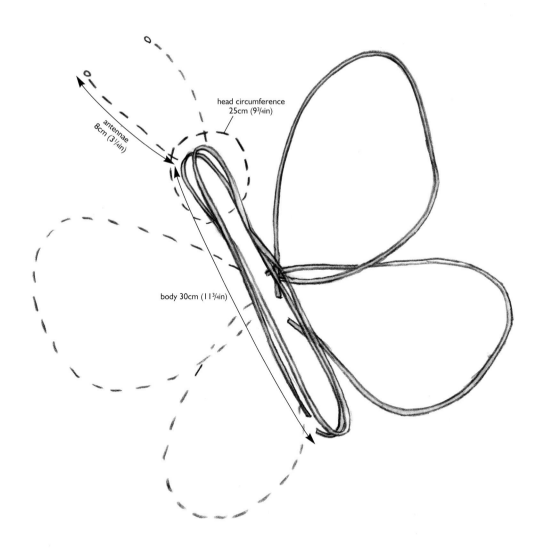

antennae
8cm (3¼in)

head circumference
25cm (9¾in)

body 30cm (11¾in)

Hanging Baskets

Hand woven hanging baskets can brighten up any garden when filled with colour. Here, one of the baskets is woven using traditional methods, the other is modern and stylish. Both are lined with brown coconut fibre and planted with summer flowers. These baskets would look wonderful hanging in a conservatory or decorating a peaceful arbor.

Materials

¼ bundle of rods, 120cm (47¼in)
¼ bundle of rods, 175cm (69in)
Brown coconut fibre
Pliable metal
Thick electrical wire
Garden wire
Glue gun
plastic lining

Open basket

See page 18, use materials as above, plus:
Larger ring, circumference 60cm (23½in)
Smaller ring, circumference 47cm (18½in)

Closed Basket

This basket does not use the normal woven ring as a base. Lay two 175cm (69in) rods together, thick ends against thin ends and twist them around each other. Repeat this process three more times, so you have four twisted lengths of willow. Now bend them in two upwards to form the basket shape shown in the photograph and gather the ends together at the top. Secure them with garden wire. Weave 120cm (47¼in) rods into the structure from the base up, until the weaving measures 13cm (5in), see below. Finish off as described on page 18.

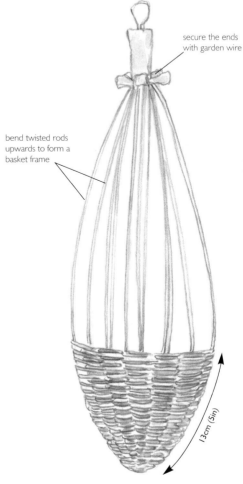

secure the ends with garden wire

bend twisted rods upwards to form a basket frame

13cm (5in)

Open Basket

Next, follow the method on page 17 and make the basket with four lengths of twisted 175cm (69in) rods. After securing the top with garden wire, the two woven circles which form the body of the basket can be attached to the frame (see right). To make the two circles, lay two 120cm (47^1/$_4$in) rods together, thick ends against thin ends and twist them around each other. Make one with a circumference of 60cm (23^1/$_2$in) and the other with a circumference of 47cm (18^1/$_2$in). Secure both in the centre with garden wire.

Wrap the smaller ring around the basket, 10cm (4in) up from the base, and secure with garden wire in two places. To make the structure really firm, zig zag a thin 120cm (47^1/$_4$in) rod around the ring (see diagram page 35). This will maintain the equal distances between the upright rods. Place the larger ring 20cm (8in) up from the base and repeat the process, weaving a thin rod in and around the upright rods. Finish the basket as described below.

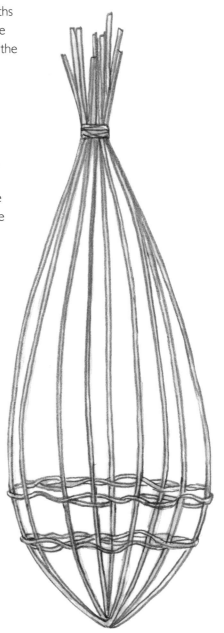

Finishing off

To make a hanging loop, weave electrical wire into the top of the basket. The loop should measure 20cm (8in). Weave rods in and around the loop and the top of the basket. Make sure they are firmly attached together. Cut out a 10 x 10cm (4 x 4in) square of pliable metal and mould this around the join (see photograph). Secure in place using a glue gun.

Now cut a strip of pliable metal, 90cm (35^1/$_2$in) long x 1cm (^{1}/$_2$in) wide and position it along the bottom edge of the moulded metal in gentle waves (see photograph). Secure with garden wire.

Finally, fill the baskets with coconut fibre, and line the insides with plastic to prevent leakage. Fill the baskets with earth and flowers, allowing some of the leaves to hang over the edges.

It is easy to make different sized baskets using the techniques shown here. Just adjust the size of the rods. Many beautiful effects can be created by displaying multi-coloured arrangements in small, medium and large baskets.

Dogs

These dogs add charm and interest to a quiet spot in the orchard. They will bring a smile to visitors' faces if you place them by your front door with a notice saying "Beware of the dogs".

Large Dog

Body and head

Refer to the Materials list and make eight woven rings (see page 5). Form two middle ovals and a bottom oval for the body frame. Slide the four inner rings (see diagram opposite), into the three body ovals. Bind them together with garden wire. Add the the top ring and bind it to the body frame. Weave rods into the whole body frame, leaving the top ring open for the head. Secure four rods at even intervals on to this top edge. These form the head, but they also form the legs. Position them to form a frame for the head which will be 16cms (6¼in) in length, and a frame for the legs which will should be pushed into the body 15cm (6in) below the head. Slide the two rings for the head on to the head rods and secure them with garden wire. Now weave rods into the whole head frame, bending them slightly towards the nose.

Materials

¼ bundle of rods, 175cm (69in)
½ bundle of rods, 120cm (47¼in)
Thick electrical wire
Garden wire

Body

Front inner ring, circumference 130cm (51¼in)
Middle inner ring, circumference 110cm (43¼in)
Back inner ring, circumference 85cm (33½in)
Back inner ring, circumference 45cm (17¾in)
Top ring, circumference 50cm (19¾in)
Middle oval, circumference 70cm (27½in)
Middle oval, circumference 85cm (33½in)
Bottom oval, circumference 85cm (33½in)

Head

Head ring, round, circumference 40cm (15¾in)
Front ring, round, circumference 35cm (13¾in)

Front legs

4 rings, round, circumference 10cm (4in)

Ears

2 rings, 38cm (15in) (see diagram opposite)

Legs

Secure the four rods to the body, making sure that the legs are positioned 15cms (6in) away from the head. The legs should be the length of the body. To form the frame for one leg, slide two leg rings over two rods, with the smaller ring forming the paw. Secure with garden wire and weave rods into the frame. Weave under the paws a little to the front to make a paw with toes. Make the other one in the same way.

Back legs

For each back leg, insert a rod into the rear of the body and bring it out to the side 30cms (11¾in) along, then form an oval and secure it to the body (see diagram). Repeat the process and place another rod in front of the first one. Weave rods into and around the leg to create a realistic shape.

Ears

Two woven circles form the ears. which are slightly shaped into ovals. Weave rods into the frames and secure them to the head with one rod, so they protrude about 10cm (4in).

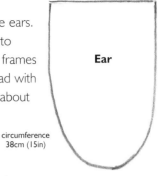

Ear

circumference
38cm (15in)

Tail

Using a 35cm (13¾in) length of electrical wire, secure 5cm (2in) to the body and wrap rods around the remaining length. Bend the tail (see photograph opposite) and secure it to the body.

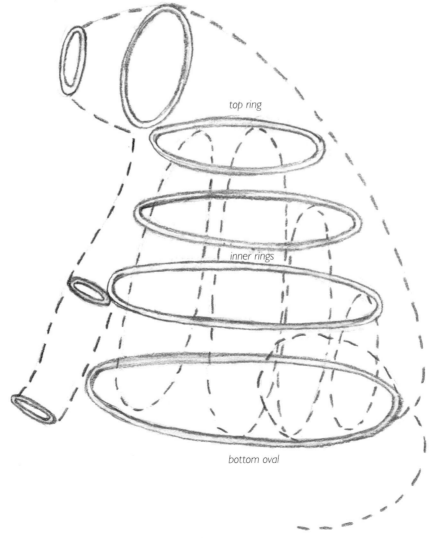

top ring

inner rings

bottom oval

Small Dog

Body and head

Refer to the Materials list and make the woven rings (see page 5). Slide the three inner body rings into the three body ovals (see diagram below), and secure them with garden wire. Add the top ring and bind it to the body frame. Weave the body fully, but leave the top ring open for the head. Secure four rods round the top ring, with a 16cm (6¼in) overhang to form the head. Slide the three head rings on to the head rods, securing them with garden wire and weave the other ends into the body.

Weave the body and head fully. While forming the head, shape the nose, a topknot and two dewlaps on the underside of the head (see photograph on page 20). Referring to the diagram, cut two ears from leather and secure with garden wire under the topknot.

8cm (1½in)

21cm (8¼in)

Ear
cut two

25cm (9¾in)

Front legs

The legs are 4cm (1½in) long. Shape the two 14cm (5½in) rings into ovals. Slide two rods into each leg, secure and weave them in the body under the stomach (see photograph on page 20). Slide the 15cm (6in) rings on for the paws and secure. Weave the legs fully.

Back legs

The back legs are positioned 7cm (2¾in) below the centre back. Weave the two 14cm (5½in) upper leg rings into the body and insert two rods into each to form lower leg frames. Slide the 15cm (6in) rings on for the paws and secure. Weave the legs. The length from the body to the paws is 9cm (3½in).

Tail

Follow the instructions for the big dog. Bend the tail and secure it to the body.

Materials

½ bundle of rods, 120cm (47¼in)
Brown leather
Thick electrical wire
Garden wire

Body

Middle inner ring, circumference 53cm (21in)
Front inner ring, circumference 45cm (17¾in)
Back inner ring, circumference 50cm (19¾in)
Top oval, circumference 85cm (33½in)
Middle oval, circumference 94cm (37in)
Bottom oval, circumference 85cm (33½in)
Top ring, fastened to body,
circumference 32cm (12½in)

Legs

4 rings, circumference 14cm (5½in)
4 rings, circumference 15cm (6in)

Head

Neck ring, circumference 30cm (11¾in)
Head oval, circumference 46cm (18in)
Head ring, circumference 26cm (10¼in)

Ears

Leather, 21cm x 8cm (8¼ x 3¼in)

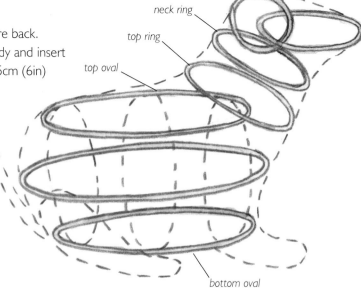

neck ring

top ring

top oval

bottom oval

22

ROCKING HORSE

Materials

Bundle of withes, 120cm (47¼in)

Thick rope, 30cm (11¾in)

Red leather harness

Metal rocker base

Thick electrical wire

Garden wire

Body

Front inner ring, circumference
60cm (23½in)

Middle inner ring, circumference
60cm (23½in)

Back inner ring, circumference
57cm (22½in)

Top oval, circumference 80cm (31½in)

Middle oval, circumference
100cm (39¼in)

Bottom oval, circumference
80cm (31½in)

Lower neck ring, fastened to body,
circumference 25cm (9¾in)

Upper neck ring, circumference
25cm (9¾in)

Legs

4 upper ovals, circumference
21cm (8¼in)

4 knee rings, circumference 18cm (7in)

4 foot rings, circumference 13cm (5in)

Head

Ring, circumference 25cm (9¾in)

Oval, circumference 36cm (14in)

Ears

2 ovals, circumference 15cm (6in)

This decorative rocking horse will delight friends and family and take you back to the golden days of your childhood. It is a wonderful project for all ages.

Body and head

Referring to the Materials list, make the basic rings (see page 5). Slide the three inner body rings into the three body ovals, securing each with garden wire (see diagram below). Secure the lower neck ring to the body frame. Weave the body fully leaving the lower neck ring open. Push four rods through the lower neck ring and body leaving an overlap to secure the upper neck and head rings. The height of the neck is 6cm (2¼in). Slide the upper neck ring and head rings into position. Weave the head and neck, then weave them securely to the body.

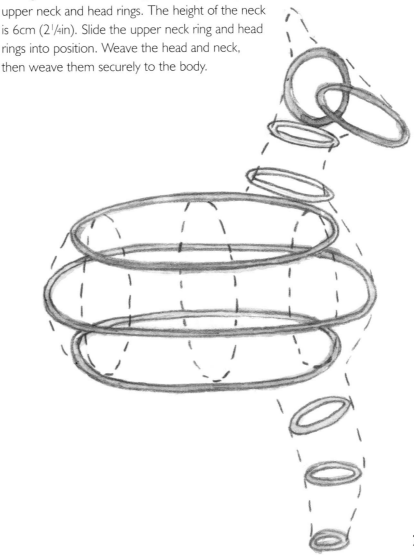

Legs

The length from the body to the knee is 11cm (4¼in). The length of the whole leg is 25cm (9¾in). Make each leg with an upper oval, a knee and a foot ring. Slot four rods through each and into the underside of the body, securing them in place. Position the back legs so that they angle away from the body. Weave the legs fully.

Ears and tail

The ears are 4cm (1½in) high and the two ovals are woven into the head. The 30cm (11¾in) tail is made from unravelled thick rope, and it is secured with garden wire. To finish off, secure the legs to the metal rocker base.

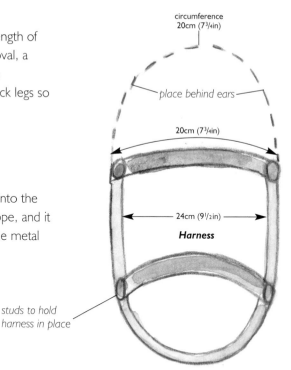

circumference
20cm (7¾in)

place behind ears

20cm (7¾in)

24cm (9½in)

Harness

studs to hold
harness in place

A simple harness has been added as a finishing touch. This can be bought, or made using strips of leather and four large studs.

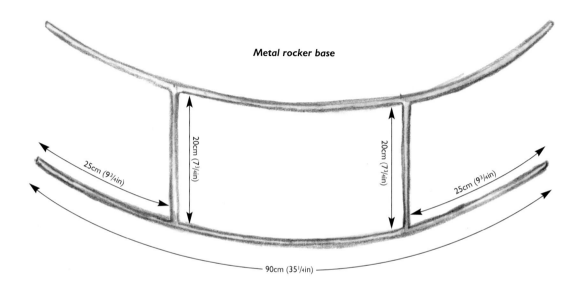

Metal rocker base

20cm (7¾in)

20cm (7¾in)

25cm (9¾in)

25cm (9¾in)

90cm (35¼in)

Doll's Prams

These eye-catching prams will look great wherever you place them. Use them as a nursery for young plants, or fill them with coconut fibre and use them for stunning flower and foliage displays throughout the seasons.

Materials

¼ bundle of rods, 120cm (47¼in)

Top edge ring, circumference 119cm (46¾in)

Small mesh chicken wire, 100 x 100cm (39¼ x 39¼in)

Moss

Metal frame with wheels

Thick electrical wire, 70cm (27½in)

Garden wire

White coconut fibre

Plants

Using a wire cutter and following the diagram below, cut the base of the pram from chicken wire 77cm (30¼in) long and 40cm (15¾in) wide. Lay moss along one half of its length, then fold the chicken wire over lengthways and secure with garden wire.

The side and side hood are cut out in one piece. Cut two from chicken wire following the diagrams on page 28. Lay one piece down flat, cover with moss, then place the other piece on top. Secure the two pieces with garden wire. Lay the hood end in position against the rectangular base and secure with garden wire in two places. Bend into place and secure with garden wire at regular intervals. Repeat for the other side.

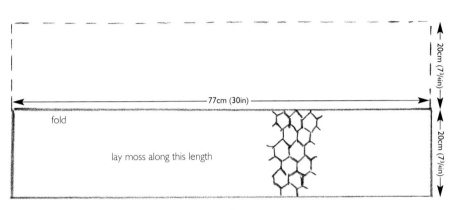

fold

lay moss along this length

77cm (30in)

20cm (7¾in)

20cm (7¾in)

Pram base

Bend the top edge ring into shape and secure with garden wire to the top edge of the pram and up around the front of the hood. Wind more rods all around this edge to secure the frame and to decorate the pram. Using garden wire, secure a rod along the bottom edge of one side of the pram, from the handle end bending it round to the top of the hood. Repeat the process on the other side. Now lay three rods along one side of the hood, to resemble spokes, and secure with garden wire. Repeat on the other side of the hood.

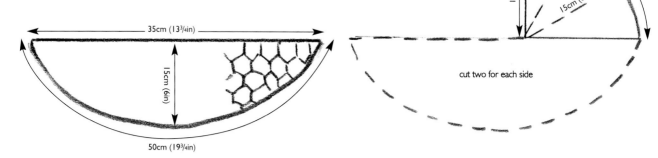

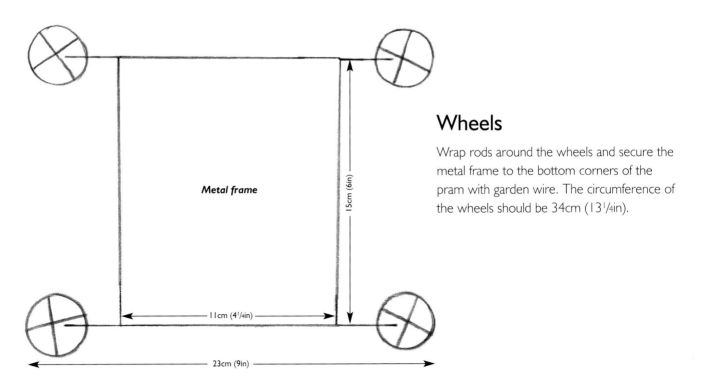

Wheels

Wrap rods around the wheels and secure the metal frame to the bottom corners of the pram with garden wire. The circumference of the wheels should be 34cm (13¹/₄in).

Metal frame

15cm (6in)

11cm (4¹/₄in)

23cm (9in)

Handle

Wrap rods around the electrical wire until you have the required thickness. Position the handle inside the pram and secure with garden wire, bending it into shape as you work along its length.

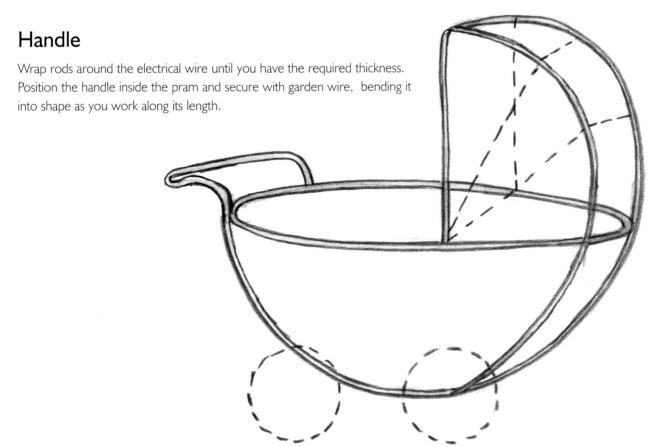

DOLPHIN IN A HOOP

Dolphins are intelligent playful, and friendly. Jumping and somersaulting, a dolphin is a decorative and entertaining feature in a garden, especially by a pond or stream.

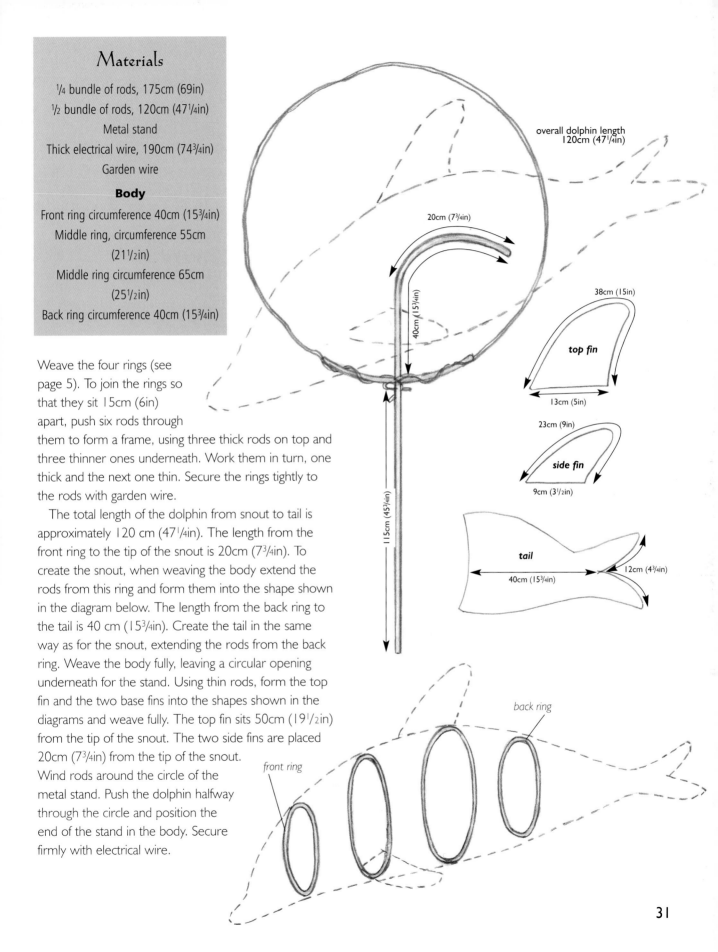

Materials

¼ bundle of rods, 175cm (69in)

½ bundle of rods, 120cm (47¼in)

Metal stand

Thick electrical wire, 190cm (74¾in)

Garden wire

Body

Front ring circumference 40cm (15¾in)

Middle ring, circumference 55cm
(21½in)

Middle ring circumference 65cm
(25½in)

Back ring circumference 40cm (15¾in)

Weave the four rings (see page 5). To join the rings so that they sit 15cm (6in) apart, push six rods through them to form a frame, using three thick rods on top and three thinner ones underneath. Work them in turn, one thick and the next one thin. Secure the rings tightly to the rods with garden wire.

The total length of the dolphin from snout to tail is approximately 120 cm (47¼in). The length from the front ring to the tip of the snout is 20cm (7¾in). To create the snout, when weaving the body extend the rods from this ring and form them into the shape shown in the diagram below. The length from the back ring to the tail is 40 cm (15¾in). Create the tail in the same way as for the snout, extending the rods from the back ring. Weave the body fully, leaving a circular opening underneath for the stand. Using thin rods, form the top fin and the two base fins into the shapes shown in the diagrams and weave fully. The top fin sits 50cm (19½in) from the tip of the snout. The two side fins are placed 20cm (7¾in) from the tip of the snout. Wind rods around the circle of the metal stand. Push the dolphin halfway through the circle and position the end of the stand in the body. Secure firmly with electrical wire.

overall dolphin length
120cm (47¼in)

20cm (7¾in)

40cm (15¾in)

115cm (45¾in)

38cm (15in)

top fin

13cm (5in)

23cm (9in)

side fin

9cm (3½in)

tail

40cm (15¾in)

12cm (4¾in)

front ring

back ring

Nesting Swans

A pair of graceful willow swans nest quietly by a garden pond. This unusual feature is a wonderful addition to a water garden, stream or tranquil area.

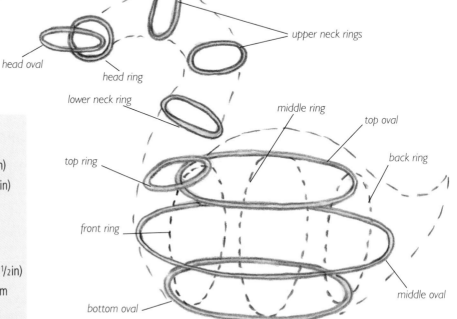

Materials

½ bundle of rods, 175cm (69in)

¼ bundle of rods, 120cm (47¼in)

Metal stand

Garden wire

Body

Front ring, circumference 85cm (33½in)

Middle ring, circumference 95cm (37½in)

Back ring, circumference 60cm (23½in)

Upper oval, circumference 95cm (37½in)

Middle oval, circumference 135cm (53in)

Bottom oval, circumference 95cm (37½in)

Neck

Top ring, fastened to body, circumference 20cm (7¾in)

Lower neck ring circumference 20cm (7¾in)

2 upper neck rings, circumference 16cm (6¼in)

Head

Head ring, 20cm (7¾in) circumference

Head oval, 27cm (10in) circumference

Body

Weave the rings (see page 5). Slide the inner front, middle and back rings into the body rings: the upper, middle and bottom ovals. Secure the body frame with garden wire. Attach the top neck ring to the body frame. Leaving this top ring open for the neck, weave the body fully and at the same time weave a point for the tail. To form the neck, push four rods in through the top ring opening allowing 40cm (15¾in) for the length of the neck. Secure them with garden wire. Slide the neck rings on to the rods and secure. Weave the neck until it is almost complete, then slide the head ring and oval into position and secure. Continue weaving until the neck and head are complete. The beak is a triangle with a base of 5cm (2in); the other two sides are 7.5cm (3in). Extend the head to form this shape.

Wings

The wings are 50cm (19½in) long from neck to tail. Push one end of a rod into the body at the base of the neck, and the other above the tail to form the top of the wing. This curves to a height of 10cm (4in) above the body. Repeat on the opposite side. Weave both wings loosely.

HANGING LAMP

A hanging lamp is beautiful in any room. This one is decorated with ivy, but you could use thin voile in a complementary colour which matches your room. For a festive variation, decorate it with fairy lights.

weave a rod in and out around the ring to make the circle secure

weave this ring 25cm (9³/₄in) above the bottom ring

5cm (2in)

9cm (3¹/₂in)

Materials

¹/₄ bundle of rods, 175cm (69in)

Ring, circumference 225cm (88¹/₂in)

Ivy

Thick brown electrical wire, 55cm (21¹/₂in)

Garden wire

First make a 125cm (49¹/₄in) circumference ring. Bind twenty-four rods together with garden wire at the top. Push the rods one by one through the ring at 9cm (3¹/₂in) intervals. The ends of the rods should protrude 5cm (2in) from the underside of the ring. Weave a rod in and out around the rods and this ring to secure the circle (see diagram above).

Now weave another ring around the lamp, 25cm (9³/₄in) above the bottom ring, (see diagram). The circumference of this ring is 95cm (37¹/₄in). Weave a rod in and out around this ring to secure the circle.

Form a knot at one end of the electrical wire. Measure 35cm (13³/₄in) from the knot and make a hanging loop. Loosen the upper binding wire and slip the knot in between the rods. Bind the rods tightly again to secure them above the knot. Bind them again in two places. Decorate the lamp with ivy.

ELEPHANT

This delightful elephant forms a central feature amongst the grasses, stones and pebbles. It would liven up any area of the garden.

Materials

Bundle of rods, 120cm (47¼in)

Thick electrical wire, 142cm (56in)

Garden wire

Body

Front inner ring, circumference 80cm (31½in)

Middle inner ring, circumference 98cm (38½in)

Back inner oval, circumference 80cm (31½in)

Top oval, circumference 82cm (32¼in)

Middle oval, circumference 82cm (32¼in)

Bottom oval, circumference 82cm (32¼in)

Head

Top oval, circumference 58cm (22¾in)

Head ring, circumference 56cm (22in)

Trunk

5th ring, circumference 41cm (16in)

4th ring, circumference 25cm (9¾in)

3rd ring, circumference 24cm (9½in)

2nd ring, circumference 24cm (9½in)

1st ring, circumference 23cm (9in)

Feet

4 top rings, circumference 29cm (11½in)

2 back base rings, circumference 32cm (12½in)

2 front base rings, circumference 34cm (13¼in)

Body and head

Make the rings (see page 5). Slide the two inner rings and one inner oval into the three body ovals. Bind the frame together with garden wire (see diagram on page 38). Attach the top head oval to the body frame with garden wire. Weave the body fully, leaving the head oval open.

Bind the head ring to the fifth trunk ring. The length from the body to the first of the trunk rings is 15 cm (6in). Push four rods into the head opening, leaving enough length showing for the 43cm (17in) trunk. Secure them with garden wire, then slide the head ring and the fifth trunk ring on to them. Secure with garden wire. Weave this section.

Slide the remaining trunk rings on to the same four rods at regular intervals and finish off by weaving the trunk fully. Shape the end of the trunk as shown in the photograph.

Legs

The legs are 15cm (6in) long and are positioned beneath the body as shown in the photograph. Push four rods into the woven frame, one for each leg. Slide each of the top rings into place, about 4cm (1½in) under the body, and secure with garden wire. Slide the base rings on, 11cm (4¼in) from the top rings, and secure them. Weave the legs fully. Remember to weave the soles of the feet closed.

Ears

Cut two 55cm (21½in) pieces of electrical wire and bend each into the shape of an ear. Wrap a rod around each one, then weave them fully. Secure the ears to the head; the distance between them is 10cm (4in). You can now bend and shape them further to complement the head and body

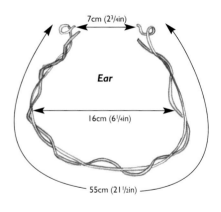

Tail

Using the remaining 32cm (12½in) of electrical wire make the tail. Wrap it with rods and secure it to the elephant with garden wire.

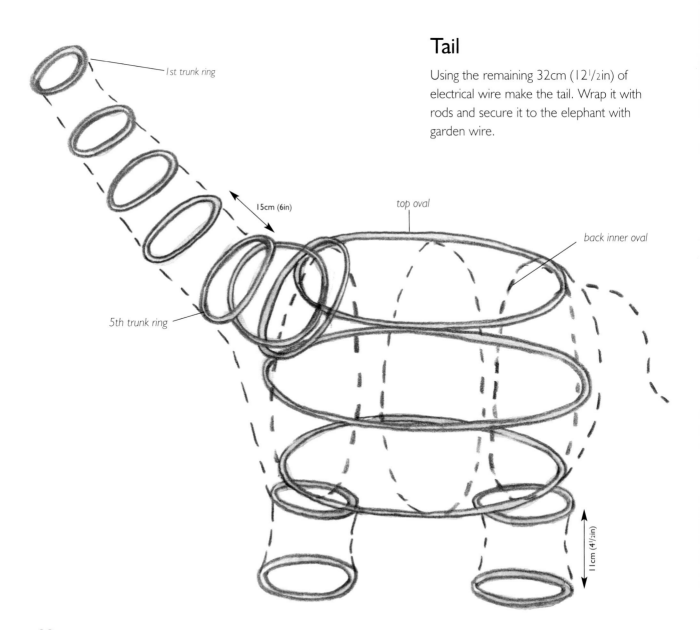

38

SAILING BOATS

There is nothing more pleasant than to sit daydreaming by the water,
watching the boats glide by.

Materials

¼ bundle of rods, 120cm (47¼in)

Top oval, circumference 90cm (35½in)

Clear polythene lining

Linen sail

Thick thread

Plywood

Garden wire

Make a rigid oval with a 90cm (35½in) circumference (see page 5). Push a 50cm (19½in) rod from the front to the back of the oval to make the curved underside of the boat. Wind a rod around it to make it firm. Push a rod from one side of the top oval through the curve of the underside and up through the other side of the top oval, to create a 'V' shape , as shown in diagram (a).

The depth in the centre of the boat is 11cm (4¼in). Repeat the 'V' with another rod close up against the first one. Allow the two rods to protrude 5cm (2in) up from the top oval and then bend them back into the top oval; do not cut them off. Repeat this twice towards the back and twice towards the front of the boat, to make a total of five double 'V' shapes.

Push a rod into the bow of the boat and weave under and over the 'V's to the back as shown in diagram (b) opposite. Now weave round the stern and back towards the bow on the other side. Repeat this process until the sides of the boat are fully worked. Trim the rod ends.

Line the inside of the boat with clear polythene. Make the deck to size from plywood and bore a hole into it for the mast. Use a rigid upright rod for the mast.

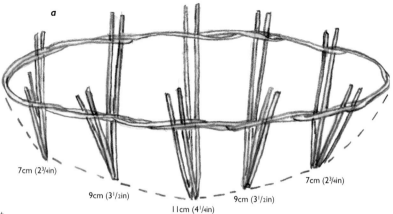

a

7cm (2¾in)

7cm (2¾in)

9cm (3½in)

9cm (3½in)

11cm (4¼in)

Make the sails as shown in diagram (c). Sew two short lengths of rod on to the top and bottom of the large bottom sail. Sew another to the bottom only of the sail above. These short lengths of rod serve to stretch the sails, which you secure to the mast and the boat with strong thread. Following the same process, secure the other two sails to the mast and boat. Finish by setting the boat on a wooden stand, see diagram (d).

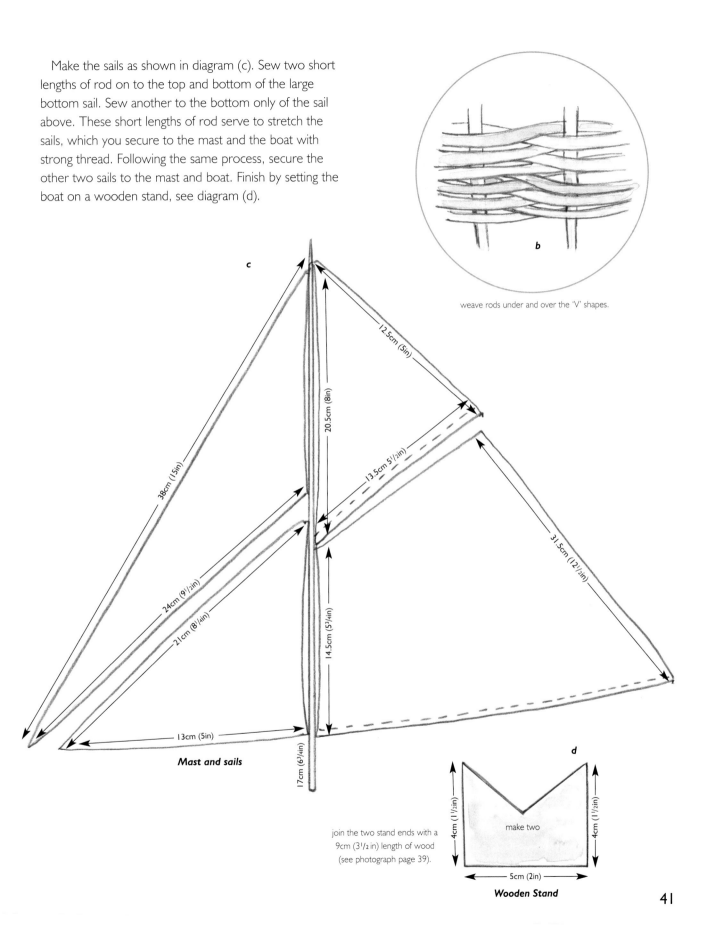

b

weave rods under and over the 'V' shapes.

c

12.5cm (5in)

20.5cm (8in)

38cm (15in)

13.5cm 5½in)

31.5cm (12½in)

24cm (9½in)

21cm (8¼in)

14.5cm (5¾in)

13cm (5in)

17cm (6¾in)

Mast and sails

d

4cm (1½in)

make two

4cm (1½in)

5cm (2in)

join the two stand ends with a 9cm (3½in) length of wood (see photograph page 39).

Wooden Stand

41

CHRISTMAS STANDS

These two decorated stands will set the scene for dinner parties and the festive season, and will give your guests a warm welcome.

Materials

¼ bundle of rods, 120cm (47¼in)
Chicken wire, 45 x 90cm (17¾ x 35½in)
100cm (39¼in) of thick green wire
Metal stand
Reel of gold wire
Assorted Christmas foliage
Fir cones
Chestnuts
Moss
Red apples
Christmas lights
Garden wire

To make one stand, cut the chicken wire to size following diagram (a), and bind the straight edges together to form the cone. Bind the top rim of the cone to the metal stand with garden wire following diagram (b) overleaf. Fill the cone with fir cones and chestnuts. Cover the bottom ring of the stand with moss and wind gold wire around to secure. Wind two rods around the bound moss. Weave green foliage around the top edge of the cone and arrange it so that it hangs down over the chicken wire. To make a wreath, bend the thick green wire into a ring then cut small bunches of Christmas foliage and secure them to the ring with a long length of garden wire; do not cut the wire, but use it continuously during this process. Lay the wreath on the top of the foliage and secure it with garden wire in several places. Make a ball of paper that will fit into the wreath and lay moss over the top. Wind gold wire around the ball to secure the moss. Lay the moss ball into the wreath and cover it with Christmas lights.

Push three rods into the moss ball so that they arch over it. To finish off, decorate with fir cones and red apples.

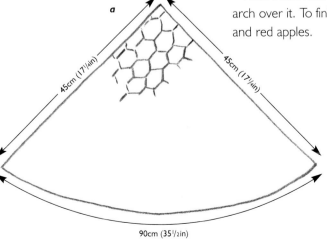

a

45cm (17¼in)

45cm (17¼in)

90cm (35½in)

b

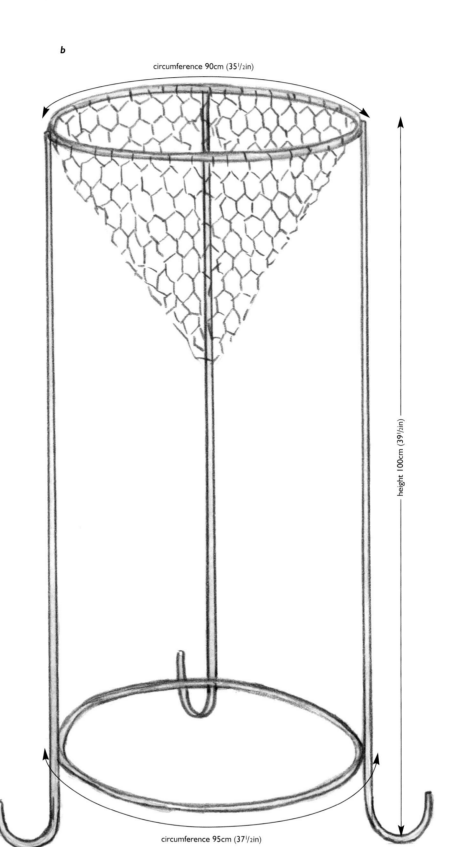

circumference 90cm (35¹/₂in)

height 100cm (39¹/₂in)

circumference 95cm (37¹/₂in)

Conclusion

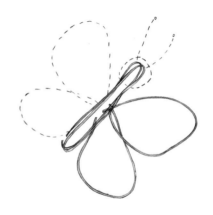

We hope that you have enjoyed making the models in this book and that you now have the skills and inspiration to start creating your own projects. We are constantly inspired by nature and the world around us, and hope you will be too. We recently visited a group in Denmark to demonstrate our weaving methods, but when they saw our stock of willow rods there was much laughter. It turned out that we had nothing new to teach them, but we did learn a lot from them – so the hanging baskets and the sailing boats are made using Danish techniques.

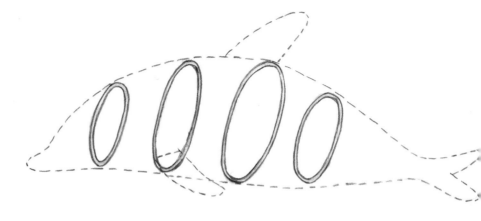